The Labradoodle Way

A Guide to Successful Dog Ownership

Gus Tales

Book Cover & Illustrations by Alrium Digital

Contents

knowledge and abilities you need to successfully navigate the rewarding journey of Labradoodle parenthood through this book.

I've collaborated with a team of experts, including cynologists, veterinarians, and specialists in canine behavior, to bring you the most accurate and helpful information we can. This manual accurately reflects a thorough and all-encompassing approach to Labradoodle ownership thanks to the extensive knowledge and experience of these experts.

The subsequent chapters provide a wealth of information on all facets of Labradoodle care, from their history and distinctive characteristics to the vital practices and rituals necessary to ensure a harmonious coexistence. This guide will walk you through choosing the ideal puppy or adopting a Labradoodle from a rescue organization, as well as how to prepare your home, establish routines, and build a strong, loving bond with your new dog friend. We'll also go into great detail regarding senior Labradoodle care, including its unique rewards and challenges, as well as suitable dietary needs, medical attention, grooming, training, physical activity, and mental stimulation.

As you embark on this exciting journey with your Labradoodle, keep in mind the importance of love, patience, and consistency at all times. These qualities will not only improve your bond with your dog, but they will also pave the way for a lifetime of happiness and understanding.

Finally, if you find "The Labradoodle Way: A Guide to Successful Dog Ownership" beneficial, I kindly ask that you consider leaving a review. Your feedback not only helps us improve, but also aids fellow Labradoodle owners in finding this resource. Thank you in advance for your support.

Together, let's embark on this amazing journey, and I wish you and your Labradoodle a lifetime of joy, amusement, and companionship. Welcome to "The Labradoodle Way."

Sincerely,
Gus Tales & Isabel the Cavapoo

CHAPTER I

The Labradoodle: A Mix of Labrador Charm and Poodle Intelligence

I f you're reading this book, there's a good chance you're inter-ested in Labradoodles or maybe you're already a proud owner of this captivating breed. Either way, this chapter will give you a comprehensive understanding of Labradoodles: their history, unique traits, why they've become so popular, and what sets them apart from other breeds.

So, let's embark on this exciting journey of exploring the Labradoodle, a delightful blend of Labrador charm and Poodle intelligence!

The Origin of Labradoodles

The Labradoodle story begins in Australia during the 1980s. Wally Conron, a breeding manager for the Royal Guide Dog Association of Australia, was tasked with a unique challenge. A woman in Hawaii needed a guide dog, but her husband was allergic to dogs. Conron had an idea: he decided to cross a Labrador Retriever, known for its excellent guide dog qualities, with a Standard Poodle, celebrated for its low-shedding coat and hypoallergenic properties. And thus, the first Labradoodle was born!

> **Did You Know?** The first-ever Labradoodle was named "Sultan," and he successfully fulfilled his duties as a guide dog for a visually impaired woman in Hawaii while being allergy-friendly for her husband.

While Conron had achieved his goal, he couldn't predict the massive wave of interest this breed would garner. However, it's crucial to note that Conron later expressed regret over creating the Labradoodle, fearing that his actions inadvertently sparked an unregulated market for designer dogs, where unethical breeding practices could thrive. But it's thanks to his original idea that many families worldwide can enjoy the companionship of this lovable breed.

Understanding the Different Labradoodle Generations

Now, if you're new to the world of Labradoodles, the terminology can seem a bit daunting, especially when you hear terms like F1, F1b, F2, and so on. These are generation labels that tell you more about a Labradoodle's lineage:

– F1 Labradoodle: This is the first generation, a direct cross between a purebred Labrador Retriever and a purebred Poodle. An F1 Labradoodle is typically 50% Labrador and 50% Poodle.

– F1b Labradoodle: This generation occurs when an F1 Labradoodle is bred with a purebred Poodle. F1b Labradoodles are 75% Poodle, making them more likely to have hypoallergenic and non-shedding traits.

– F2 Labradoodle: This generation is the result of two F1 Labradoodles breeding. An F2 Labradoodle can have a wide variety of traits, as their genetic makeup can lean more toward the Labrador or the Poodle.

– F2b and beyond: As you continue breeding F1 or F1b Labradoodles with either F1, F1b, or purebred Poodles, you get into F2b and further generations.

Why does this matter? Depending on what you want in a Labradoodle, understanding the generations can be crucial. If you're looking for a dog that's hypoallergenic, a higher generation Labradoodle (more Poodle genetics) may be a better fit.

Physical Traits, Temperament, and Intelligence

Labradoodles are a striking breed, exhibiting a blend of the best traits from their parent breeds. Their size can range from small to large, largely dependent on the Poodle parent (Standard, Miniature, or Toy). An average Labradoodle will typically weigh between 15 to 30 kilograms (33 to 66 pounds) and can stand anywhere from 35 to 60 centimeters (14 to 24 inches) tall.

One of the most captivating features of a Labradoodle is their coat. It can vary significantly, ranging from wiry hair to soft, dense wool, to long, flowing fleece, in colors from chalk to cafe, gold to red, black to blue. The grooming needs of a Labradoodle can depend heavily on their coat type, something we'll delve deeper into in a later chapter.

> Tip: When choosing your Labradoodle, ask the breed-er about the coat types of the parent dogs to get an idea of your puppy's potential coat characteristics and grooming needs.

When it comes to temperament, Labradoodles are known for their sociability, intelligence, and generally amiable nature. They carry the Labrador's reputation for friendliness and eagerness to please, combined with the Poodle's known intelligence and trainability. This makes them not only great family pets but also a popular choice for service and therapy roles.

Labradoodles are active and playful dogs, so they'll need plenty of exercise and mental stimulation. They're usually great with children and can get along well with other animals, especially if properly socialized (more on that in a later chapter).

The Rise of Labradoodles as Popular Family Pets

The popularity of Labradoodles has soared over the past decades. This surge in popularity is not just because of their charming looks but also their incredible versatility and the numerous benefits of owning one. Their low-shedding traits make them suitable for allergy sufferers, while their sociable and trainable nature makes them a fantastic family pet. Plus, their energy and playfulness make them a delightful companion for those with an active lifestyle.

Another crucial factor contributing to their popularity is the concept of hybrid vigor - the idea that crossbred dogs, like Labradoodles, are generally healthier and live longer than their purebred counterparts. This is due to the increased genetic diversity reducing the risk of inherited genetic disease.

Labradoodles in Various Roles

Aside from being lovable pets, Labradoodles often excel in various specialized roles thanks to their intelligence, trainability, and friendly disposition. They're known to make excellent therapy and service dogs, providing support and assistance to those in need. Additionally, they're a popular choice in various dog sports, including agility, obedience, and rally competitions, showcasing their incredible intelligence and eager-to-please nature.

In Closing

As we reach the end of this chapter, it's clear that the Labradoodle is a truly unique breed, offering a blend of intelligence, charm, versatility, and companionship that few other breeds can match. Whether you're seeking a family pet, a therapy or service dog, or simply a loyal companion, the Labradoodle can fit the bill perfectly. Their fascinating history, combined with their exceptional qualities, makes them a breed worth knowing and loving.

In the following chapters, we'll explore more about choosing the right Labradoodle, preparing for their arrival, training, care, and so much more. So stick with us, whether you're a prospective Labradoodle owner or already enjoying life with this fantastic breed. There's so much more to learn and love about the Labradoodle way!

CHAPTER 2

Choosing Your Labradoodle: Breeder, Adoption, and Selection Tips

Picking the Perfect Labradoodle for You

As with any major life decision, bringing a Labradoodle into your life requires careful consideration and thoughtful preparation. In this chapter, we delve into the essentials of choosing your furry companion, from identifying reputable breeders to selecting the perfect puppy that suits your lifestyle.

Reputable Breeders Vs. Unethical Ones

Labradoodles are a popular breed, which unfortunately means that they can sometimes be targeted by unethical breeders or 'puppy mills.' Recognizing the difference between a responsible breeder and an unethical one is critical in ensuring you get a healthy, well-adjusted Labradoodle.

A reputable breeder prioritizes the health, temperament, and quality of their dogs over profit. They have in-depth knowledge about Labradoodles and are more than willing to share this with potential buyers. They'll happily show you around their breeding facilities, which should be clean and well-maintained. Reputable breeders test their breeding dogs for genetic diseases common in Labradoodles, such as hip dysplasia and progressive retinal atrophy (PRA). This information should be readily available to you.

On the other hand, unethical breeders or 'puppy mills' prioritize profit over the well-being of their dogs. They may breed dogs in poor conditions, provide minimal veterinary care, and have little interest in the dogs' long-term health and well-being. Puppies from these facilities often have behavioral and health issues, some of which may not become apparent until later in life.

Tip: Ask for proof of health screenings for the parents of your prospective Labradoodle puppy. A reputable breeder will gladly provide this.

Questions to Ask a Breeder or Rescue Organization

When you've identified a potential breeder, prepare a list of questions to ensure they're the right fit. Here are a few key questions to ask:

* Can I visit the puppies and their parents? A good breeder will encourage you to visit.

* Have the puppies been socialized? Early socialization is key to a well-adjusted Labradoodle.

* Can you provide references from previous buyers or the breeder's veterinarian?

* Are the puppies' parents tested for genetic diseases?

* What guarantees do you provide in terms of health and temperament?

If you're adopting from a rescue organization, you should ask about the dog's history, behavior, and any known health issues. It's also essential to ask how the organization evaluates dogs for adoption and what support they provide to adopters.

Evaluating a Labradoodle's Health and Temperament

When selecting your Labradoodle, health and temperament are two critical factors to consider. A healthy puppy should be alert and active, with clear eyes and nose, and a clean, shiny coat. They should be comfortable with being handled and show no signs of discomfort or fear.

Evaluate the puppy's temperament by observing how they interact with their littermates and with you. Is the puppy confident and curious, or are they nervous and fearful? A well-socialized Labradoodle puppy should be outgoing and eager to interact with people.

It's essential to remember that while physical health is important, mental health is equally crucial. Look for signs of a balanced temperament: a puppy that's neither too shy nor overly dominant.

> Did you know? The temperament of a Labradoodle can vary depending on whether it's an F1, F1B, or F2 generation. F1 and F2 Labradoodles typically exhibit a balanced blend of the Labrador and Poodle temperaments, while F1B Labradoodles may lean more towards the Poodle temperament, which can be a little more reserved.

Choosing a Labradoodle to Fit Your Lifestyle

Not every Labradoodle will be the right fit for every home. Consider your lifestyle, including your living situation, work schedule, and activity level. Labradoodles require a fair amount of exercise and mental stimulation, so they're better suited to active families or individuals who enjoy outdoor activities.

Labradoodles come in various sizes, from miniatures that weigh between 15–30 pounds (7–14 kg) to standards that can weigh 50–65 pounds (23–29 kg). Make sure you choose a size that fits well with your living situation.

> Fun Fact: Despite their size, Labradoodles are known for being great "lap dogs," loving nothing more than cuddling up with their favorite humans!

Early Socialization for Labradoodles

Early socialization is crucial for Labradoodles. Socialized puppies are more likely to grow up into confident, well-adjusted dogs. They should be exposed to a variety of people, environments, and other animals from a young age. A reputable breeder will start this process, but it's up to you to continue it once the puppy comes home.

Spotting Potential Red Flags

Be aware of red flags when visiting breeders or rescue organizations. Some signs of concern include:

* Unwillingness to let you meet the puppy's parents
* Puppies kept in dirty or crowded conditions
* Puppies that seem fearful, anxious, or excessively shy
* Lack of veterinary records or proof of health screenings

* The breeder has multiple litters available and seems more focused on making a sale than finding good homes for their puppies

The Role of Adoption and Rescue

Adoption is a wonderful way to bring a Labradoodle into your life. Many wonderful Labradoodles are in need of loving homes. Rescue organizations and shelters typically have adult dogs, but sometimes they have puppies as well. Adopting an adult Labradoodle has its advantages. They're often already house-trained and socialized, and their personality is fully developed, so there are fewer surprises down the road.

Preparing Your Home and Existing Pets

Bringing a new Labradoodle home is an exciting event, but it's important to prepare your home and any existing pets for the new arrival. Ensure your home is safe for a curious puppy by removing any toxic plants and securing loose wires or other potential hazards. If you have other pets, introduce them to the new puppy gradually and under supervision to ensure a smooth transition.

A Labradoodle for Life

Bringing a Labradoodle into your life is a long-term commitment. This energetic, intelligent, and affectionate breed can bring immense joy and companionship into your home. By doing your research and making an informed choice, you're taking the first step towards a rewarding relationship with your new furry friend. And remember, owning a Labradoodle is not just about the cute puppy phase – you're in for a lifetime of wet noses, wagging tails, and unconditional love.

Next, we'll talk about how to prepare for your Labradoodle's arrival – from setting up the perfect sleeping spot to choosing the best toys for stimulation and play. So, stay tuned and get ready to be the best Labradoodle parent you can be!

CHAPTER 3

Preparing for Your Labradoodle: Essential Supplies and Home Setup

Getting Ready for Your Furry Friend

C ongratulations! You've made the exciting decision to welcome a Labradoodle into your home. This hybrid breed,
boasting a mix of Labrador Retriever and Poodle genes, is known
for its affable nature, playful energy, and stunning coats. But

before your Labradoodle bounds through your front door, there are a few essential things you need to prepare.

Thomas Campbell, an acclaimed poet, once said, "Coming events cast their shadows before." In a similar vein, the arrival of a new pet in the household often brings about some changes. For your Labradoodle to feel truly at home, it's important to make these changes in advance.

> Did you know? Labradoodles are known for their so-ciable nature and thrive in environments where they feel loved and included.

Identifying and Removing Potential Hazards

Think of your home from a puppy's point of view – there are so many exciting things to explore! However, what appears harmless to us might pose a risk to a curious Labradoodle. It's crucial to puppy-proof your home, much like you would for a toddler. Here's how you can create a safe environment:

1. Toxic Plants: Many houseplants are poisonous to dogs. Common plants like Sago Palm, Azaleas, and English Ivy can be harmful. Be sure to check if your plants are safe for dogs and, if not, place them out of reach.

2. Small Objects: Labradoodles, especially puppies, love to chew on things. Small objects like coins, buttons, or toy parts can be a choking hazard. Ensure these are stored securely.

3. Wires and Cords: Electrical wires and cords can be tempting chew toys. Use cord protectors or keep them hidden away.

4. Cleaning Supplies: Most cleaning products are toxic if ingested. Store these in locked cabinets.

5. Medicines and Cosmetics: These items can be harmful or fatal if ingested. Keep them in closed cabinets that your Labradoodle can't access.

6. Trash Cans: Dogs often rummage in the trash, which can be dangerous. Invest in a dog-proof trash can or store it out of sight.

Tip: Use a baby gate to keep your Labradoodle away from potentially dangerous areas like staircases or rooms with many hazards.

Designing Spaces: Crate, Bed, and Feeding Area

The next step in preparing for your Labradoodle is creating designated spaces for sleeping, feeding, and downtime.

The Crate

A crate is more than a training tool; it's a safe haven for your dog. Dogs are den animals, and a crate simulates this natural environment. It offers a secure, cozy place where your Labradoodle can relax.

While some people might see crates as cruel or akin to a prison, when used correctly, a crate can provide a realm of comfort and safety for your Labradoodle.

> Fact: Dogs naturally avoid soiling their sleeping area, making a crate an excellent tool for house training.

When selecting a crate, consider the size of your full-grown Labradoodle. A medium to large-sized crate, approximately 36 to 42 inches (91 to 107 cm) long, is generally ideal. However, for a puppy, you might want to start with a smaller size or use a crate with a divider that can be adjusted as your Labradoodle grows.

The crate should be large enough for your Labradoodle to stand, turn around, and lie down comfortably. But remember, if the crate is too large, your Labradoodle might use one corner as a bathroom, which defeats the purpose of crate training.

For a bed within the crate, choose something comfortable but not too plush. Many puppies go through a chewing phase, and you wouldn't want a costly bed destroyed.

The Bed

Outside the crate, it's great to have a dedicated bed where your Labradoodle can relax during the day. The location of the bed should be in a quiet, draft-free area.

As for the type of bed, Labradoodles, with their dense coats, are prone to overheating. A cot-style bed that allows airflow could be a good option, but a padded bed is also fine. As with the crate bed, keep in mind that your Labradoodle might chew it, especially during the puppy stage.

The Feeding Area

The feeding area should be in a quiet, low-traffic area where your Labradoodle can eat without being disturbed. A mat under the food and water bowls can help to catch spills.

For the food and water dishes, stainless steel or ceramic bowls are better than plastic, which can harbor bacteria and cause allergies in some dogs.

Selecting Toys and Chew Items

One of the pure joys of having a Labradoodle is watching them play. Toys and chew items are not just sources of entertainment for your Labradoodle; they also contribute to mental stimulation and dental health.

When choosing toys, make sure they're size-appropriate. Small toys can be a choking hazard for large dogs. Moreover, ensure the toys are dog-safe. Many children's toys have small parts that can be chewed off and swallowed. Dog-specific toys are designed with a dog's behavior in mind and are generally safe.

Labradoodles, like many breeds, love to chew. Chewing helps puppies soothe teething discomfort and helps adult dogs keep their jaws strong and teeth clean. Choose chew items that are safe and healthy. Some options include durable rubber toys, bully sticks, and dental chews.

> Fact: Dogs have a chewing peak at around 16–20 weeks of age. After this period, while they'll still love to chew, it won't be as intense.

Preparing an Outdoor Area

Labradoodles are active and social dogs, and an outdoor space where they can run, play, and explore is ideal. If you have a yard, check for gaps in fences or gates that a curious Labradoodle could squeeze through.

If you live in an apartment or lack a fenced yard, don't worry! Regular walks and trips to the dog park can keep your Labradoodle happy and healthy.

> Tip: If your Labradoodle will be spending a significant amount of time outdoors, provide a shady area and fresh water to prevent overheating.

Introducing Your Labradoodle to Their New Home

Introducing your Labradoodle to their new home is a process that should be done with patience and care.

When you first bring your Labradoodle home, let them explore under your supervision. Show them their crate, bed, and feeding area. Introduce them to their toys and spend some time playing together.

Keep the environment calm and quiet for the first few days to avoid overwhelming your new pet. Gradually introduce them to new people and experiences as they grow more comfortable in their new home.

Final Thoughts

The preparation phase before bringing home a new pet might seem daunting, but remember, the effort you put in now will result in a smoother transition for both you and your Labradoodle. As with anything, preparation is key, and by following the tips in this chapter, you'll be well on your way to creating a safe, comfortable, and loving environment for your new Labradoodle.

CHAPTER 4

Welcoming Your Labradoodle Home: The First Week and Beyond

The wait is over, and the day has finally arrived! Your furry friend is on their way to your home. The preparation phase is done, and now it's time to welcome your Labradoodle into their new home.

The first week with your Labradoodle will be filled with many "firsts," new experiences, and a lot of learning - for both you and your new pet. It's a time of excitement, exploration, bonding, and certainly some challenges. This chapter will guide you through that first week and set the stage for the weeks and months to follow.

As Leo F. Buscaglia, an American author, once said, "Change is the end result of all true learning." Bringing a Labradoodle into your life is a change - a wonderful one - and your journey of learning and growing together starts now.

Did you know? Labradoodles have a lifespan of around 10-15 years. These years will be filled with love, companionship, and a myriad of shared experiences.

Day 1: Arrival and Introduction

The day you bring your Labradoodle home will be filled with a mix of emotions - excitement, joy, anticipation, and maybe a bit of apprehension. Remember, your Labradoodle will be experiencing similar feelings, so it's important to make their transition as smooth as possible.

Before your Labradoodle arrives, prepare their crate, set up their bed, organize the feeding area, and ensure toys and chew items are accessible. Here are some tips for the first day:

Arrival

When you first bring your Labradoodle home, keep the environment calm and quiet. Limit the number of people present to avoid overwhelming your new pet. Remember, your Labradoodle is leaving their familiar environment, possibly for the first time, and coming to a completely new place.

Exploration

Let your Labradoodle explore their new home under your supervision. Keep an eye on them to ensure they're safe and not getting into anything harmful. Allow them to sniff around, get familiar with their surroundings, and slowly understand that this is their new home.

Introduction to Spaces

Introduce your Labradoodle to their crate, bed, and feeding area. It might take them some time to get accustomed to these spaces. Encourage them gently, and remember not to force anything. Everything is new to them, so patience is key.

Feeding

Before you bring your Labradoodle home, find out what food they were eating at the breeder's or shelter. It's recommended to continue with the same diet initially to avoid stomach upset. If you decide to switch to a different diet, do so gradually over a week or two, mixing increasing amounts of the new food with the old.

Bedtime

The first night can be challenging as your Labradoodle might feel alone and scared. If you've opted for crate training, encourage your Labradoodle to sleep in their crate. You might consider keeping the crate in your bedroom for the first few nights to provide a sense of safety and comfort.

Week 1: Setting a Routine, Bonding, and Beginning Training

After the excitement of the first day, you can start setting a routine for your Labradoodle. This week will also involve plenty of bonding time and the beginning of basic training.

Establishing a Routine

Dogs thrive on routine. A predictable schedule makes them feel secure and helps with training. Your routine should include time for meals, toilet breaks, playtime, training, and rest. Young puppies usually eat three to four times a day, while adult dogs generally eat twice a day.

Ensure that you take your Labradoodle out for toilet breaks regularly. Puppies especially have small bladders and will need to go out frequently, including shortly after meals, after they wake up, and during and after playtime.

Bonding Time

Spend quality time with your Labradoodle to strengthen your bond. This can include gentle playtime, petting, talking to them, or just sitting with them. Remember, the goal is to make your Labradoodle feel secure and loved in their new home.

Basic Training

You can begin basic training as soon as your Labradoodle comes home. Start with simple commands like "sit," "stay," "come," and "down." Use positive reinforcement like treats, praise, and petting to reward your Labradoodle when they follow a command.

Training sessions for young puppies should be short but frequent, as puppies have a short attention span. Even a few minutes of training at a time can be very effective. For older dogs, sessions can be longer, but always aim to keep training positive and fun.

Did you know? Labradoodles are intelligent and usually respond well to training. Consistency, patience, and positive reinforcement are keys to successful training.

Weeks 2 and Beyond: Socialization, Continued Training, and Health Care

After the first week, your Labradoodle will likely be more set-tled and comfortable in their new home. This is an excellent time to start introducing new people, experiences, and environments. This is also a crucial time for continued training and ensuring your Labradoodle's health care needs are met.

Socialization

Socialization involves introducing your Labradoodle to a vari-ety of people, environments, sounds, and experiences. This helps them become a well-adjusted, confident adult dog. While social-ization should continue throughout your Labradoodle's life, the primary socialization period for dogs is between 3 and 16 weeks of age.

Introduce your Labradoodle to new people gently and allow them to approach at their own pace. It's also important to expose them to various environments, such as busy streets, quiet parks, and different types of buildings and vehicles.

Remember to keep socialization experiences positive. Never force your Labradoodle into a situation that scares them. Instead, use treats and praise to create positive associations.

Continued Training

As your Labradoodle gets older, you can start teaching more complex commands and tricks. You might also consider enrolling in a puppy class or basic obedience class. These classes can be a great way to reinforce training, provide socialization opportuni-ties, and get advice from professional trainers.

Health Care

Make sure you've found a local vet and schedule your Labradoodle's first check-up, usually within the first week of bringing them home. The vet will check your Labradoodle's health and discuss vaccination schedules, flea and tick prevention, and neutering/spaying if this hasn't been done already.

The Months Ahead: Growing Together

As weeks turn into months, you and your Labradoodle will continue to learn and grow together. Training will become more advanced, and your bond will deepen. Your Labradoodle will grow physically, and their personality will shine through.

Remember, each Labradoodle is unique. Some might be outgoing and confident, while others might be more reserved. Love and accept your Labradoodle for who they are. They're not just a pet but a beloved member of your family.

Final Thoughts

The journey you've begun with your Labradoodle is a long and rewarding one. It will have its ups and downs, but the love, companionship, and joy that a Labradoodle brings are immeasurable.

As you and your Labradoodle embark on this journey, remember the words of Roger Caras, a wildlife photographer and writer,
"Dogs are not our whole life, but they make our lives whole." Your
Labradoodle has started making your life whole. Enjoy every
moment of this wonderful journey!

CHAPTER 5

Puppy Essentials: Socialization, House Training, and Early Care

B ringing home a Labradoodle puppy is an exciting time, filled with new experiences and boundless enthusiasm. These bundles of energy are eager to explore their world, and it's our job as responsible owners to guide them through this crucial developmental stage. In this chapter, we'll cover the essentials of socialization, house training, and early care.

The Critical Role of Early Socialization

"Whoever said you can't buy happiness forgot about puppies."
– Gene Hill

You may be asking, "What is socialization, and why is it so crucial for my Labradoodle puppy?"

Socialization is the process of exposing your puppy to various people, environments, sounds, smells, and experiences, all with the aim of helping them become well-adjusted and confident adults.

Did you know that puppies have a 'golden socialization period'? This period typically lasts from about three weeks to about sixteen weeks of age. During this window, puppies are most receptive to new experiences, and they'll often approach them with curiosity rather than fear.

When socializing your Labradoodle puppy, you'll want to ensure experiences are positive and not overwhelming. Regularly introduce them to different environments, people of all ages, other friendly dogs, and even other pet species if possible. Remember to keep these interactions controlled and positive, rewarding your puppy with praise, treats, and lots of love.

Setting Up a Successful Toilet Training Schedule

House training, or toilet training, is one of the first and most important lessons your Labradoodle puppy will learn. This process can take some time and patience, but with consistency and positive reinforcement, your puppy will soon understand where it's appropriate to go potty.

Start by establishing a regular feeding schedule. What goes in on a schedule will come out on a schedule. Young puppies will need to go to the bathroom frequently as their bladders are still small, often within 5–30 minutes of eating.

Take your puppy outside regularly throughout the day, especially after meals, naps, and play sessions. Always take them to the same spot. The scent will remind them of what they're there for.

When they do their business in the right place, lavish them with praise and a treat. This positive reinforcement will help them understand that going potty outside is a good thing.

> Remember, accidents will happen, especially in the early days. When they do, clean up thoroughly to remove the scent and discourage them from returning to the same spot. Avoid scolding your puppy for accidents; they're learning, and negative reactions can lead to confusion or fear.

Understanding Labradoodle Growth Stages and Developmental Milestones

As a cross between a Poodle and a Labrador Retriever, Labradoodles are considered medium to large-sized dogs. Here's a general guide to what you can expect as they grow, remembering that individual dogs may vary.

* 8 Weeks: Labradoodle puppies are typically weaned from their mother and ready to go to their new home. They will weigh around 5–10 pounds (2–4.5 kg).

* 4 Months: Your Labradoodle is now a lively, active puppy who loves to play and explore. They will weigh between 25–30 pounds (11–14 kg).

* 6 Months: At this age, your Labradoodle will start to look more like an adult dog but will still have a puppy's boundless energy. They will weigh between 35–45 pounds (16–20 kg).

* 1 Year: Congratulations, you now have an adolescent Labradoodle! They will weigh between 45–60 pounds (20–27 kg) and will be physically mature, but mentally they're still playful puppies.

Always remember to take your Labradoodle to regular veterinary check-ups to ensure they are growing healthily.

The Role of Play in a Labradoodle's Learning and Social Development

Playtime isn't just about fun; it's also a valuable learning opportunity for your Labradoodle puppy. Through play, they learn important social skills, build confidence, and burn off energy.

Engaging in different types of play such as fetch, hide and seek, or puzzle toys can also help stimulate your puppy's mind and encourage problem-solving skills. Remember to balance active play with periods of rest to prevent your puppy from becoming overtired.

Tackling Common Puppy Challenges

All puppies, Labradoodles included, will exhibit some challenging behaviors as they navigate through their early months. Here are a few common challenges and how to manage them:

* Chewing: Chewing is a normal behavior for teething puppies. Provide safe chew toys to satisfy this natural urge. If your puppy chews on an inappropriate item, redirect them to a suitable toy.

* Nipping: Puppies explore the world with their mouths, and nipping can be a common issue. Teach your Labradoodle that nipping is not acceptable by redirecting them to a toy or stopping play if they nip.

* Jumping Up: Labradoodles are enthusiastic dogs, and jumping up can be their way of saying hello. To discourage this behavior, ignore your puppy when they jump up and only give them attention when all four paws are on the ground.

With patience, consistency, and positive reinforcement, your Labradoodle will learn to replace these behaviors with more desirable ones.

Utilizing Crate Training

Crate training can be a valuable tool for house training and creating a secure haven for your Labradoodle puppy. A crate can become your puppy's safe space, a place they retreat to when they need rest or feel overwhelmed.

When choosing a crate, ensure it's large enough for your puppy to stand, turn around, and lie down comfortably, but not so large that they can designate one corner as their bathroom. As your puppy grows, you may need to upgrade the size of the crate.

Start crate training gradually, introducing your puppy to the crate with positive associations. Leave the door open, place treats or toys inside, and encourage your puppy to explore at their own pace. Once they're comfortable, you can begin closing the door for short periods.

Remember, a crate should never be used as a punishment. It should always remain a positive and safe space for your Labradoodle.

Feeding a Balanced Diet for Healthy Growth

Puppies have specific nutritional needs to support their rapid growth and development. Feed your Labradoodle a high-quality puppy food that is appropriate for their size and breed. Your vet can help guide you on the right choice and feeding amounts.

Puppies should be fed multiple small meals throughout the day. Typically, a puppy aged 8-12 weeks will need 4 meals per day, decreasing to 2-3 meals per day as they get older.

Always provide fresh water and avoid feeding your Labradoodle human food, which can contain ingredients harmful to dogs.

Providing Adequate Exercise, Mental Stimulation, and Rest

Puppies are bundles of energy, but they also need plenty of rest to support their growth. A good rule of thumb for walking a puppy is 5 minutes of exercise per month of age, up to twice a day.

At three months old, your Labradoodle puppy would benefit from 15 minutes of exercise twice a day. This can be gradually increased as they grow. Also, remember to offer plenty of playtime at home.

In addition to physical exercise, your Labradoodle puppy will need mental stimulation. You can achieve this through training sessions, puzzle toys, and interactive games. These activities will also help strengthen your bond.

Despite being active, puppies need a lot of sleep—typically up to 18–20 hours a day. Ensure they have a quiet and comfortable place to rest and sleep.

By meeting your Labradoodle puppy's physical, emotional, and mental needs, you'll be paving the way for a well-rounded, happy adult dog.

CHAPTER 6

Training Basics: Commands, Behavior, and Positive Reinforcement

Training your Labradoodle not only allows for a well-behaved pet, but it also strengthens the bond between you two, fostering trust and mutual respect. This chapter dives into the essential principles of dog training, effective techniques, and specific steps to teach your Labradoodle essential commands.

Remember, training should be an enjoyable and rewarding experience for both of you. Let's get started!

Understanding Canine Behavior and Learning

Dogs, including Labradoodles, are not much different from us when it comes to learning new things. They respond well to consistency, repetition, and positive reinforcement. Dogs learn through association, they link actions with outcomes, making their learning more predictable.

Understanding your Labradoodle's natural behavior is also key. Labradoodles are known for their intelligence and eagerness to please, which makes them relatively easy to train. However, these traits can also lead to mischief if they get bored or do not receive enough mental stimulation.

> Tip: Remember to keep training sessions short, around 10–15 minutes at a time, to keep your Labradoodle's interest high. A tired dog is less likely to respond positively.

The Importance of Positive Reinforcement

Positive reinforcement is the cornerstone of modern dog training. It involves rewarding your Labradoodle when they perform a desired behavior. Rewards can be anything your dog loves – treats, toys, praise, or even a quick game.

By consistently rewarding your Labradoodle for a specific action, they begin to associate that action with positive outcomes. This motivates them to repeat the action in the future. For example, if your Labradoodle gets a treat every time they sit on command, they're likely to sit when asked in anticipation of a reward.

> Fun fact: Labradoodles, being intelligent and food-motivated, respond extremely well to positive reinforcement!

Teaching Essential Commands

When it comes to teaching your Labradoodle commands, start with the basics: "sit," "stay," "come," and "leave it." Here's a step-by-step guide on how to teach these commands:

1. Sit

* Hold a treat close to your Labradoodle's nose and slowly lift your hand up, allowing their head to follow the treat and causing their bottom to lower.

* Once they're in a sitting position, say "sit," give them the treat, and share affection.

* Repeat this sequence a few times every day until your Labradoodle masters it. Then, ask your Labradoodle to sit before mealtime, when leaving for walks, and during other situations where you'd like them calm and seated.

2. Stay

* Before attempting to teach this command, ensure your Labradoodle has mastered the "sit" command.

* First, ask your dog to "sit."

* Then, open the palm of your hand in front of you, and say "stay."

* Take a few steps back. If they stay, give them a treat. If not, patiently go back to step one. Over time, you can gradually increase the number of steps you take before giving the treat.

* Always reward your pup for staying put — even if it's just for a few seconds.

3. Come

* This command could potentially save your Labradoodle's life, helping you keep them out of trouble or bringing them back to you in case they slip out of their leash.

* Put a leash and collar on your dog. Go down to their level and say "come," while gently pulling on the leash.

* When they get to you, reward them with affection and a treat.

* Once they've mastered it with the leash, remove it — and practice the command in a safe, enclosed area.

4. Leave it

* This command helps keep your Labradoodle safe by preventing them from eating harmful things off the ground or chasing after something dangerous.

* Place a treat in both hands and show one closed fist to your dog, saying "leave it."

* Let them sniff, lick, paw, and bark to try to get it — but ignore these behaviors.

* Once they stop trying, give them the treat from the other hand.

* Repeat until your dog moves away from the first fist when you say "leave it."

* Next, only give your dog the treat when they move away from the first fist and also look up at you.

Addressing Behavioral Challenges

While Labradoodles are generally well-behaved, you might encounter behaviors such as jumping, barking, or chewing. The key to addressing these behaviors is to understand the root cause. For instance, if your Labradoodle barks excessively, it might be due to boredom, fear, or seeking attention.

For jumping, divert your Labradoodle's attention by asking them to "sit" when they jump. Reward them for sitting and not jumping. For chewing, provide enough chew toys and keep valuable items out of their reach. For excessive barking, try to identify the cause and address it accordingly. If behavioral issues persist, consider consulting with a professional dog trainer.

Leash Training

Leash training ensures pleasant walks for both you and your Labradoodle. Start by introducing your Labradoodle to the collar/harness and leash. Let them get used to wearing them in the house before taking them outside. During walks, keep the leash loose and if your dog pulls, stop walking. Only resume when they stop pulling. Reward them when they walk nicely beside you.

Training for Positive Response to Grooming and Vet Care

Your Labradoodle should also be comfortable with grooming and veterinary checks. Begin this training early by frequently handling their paws, ears, and mouth, always pairing the experience with rewards. This way, they'll be less likely to resist during grooming or vet exams.

Advanced Training Options

After mastering basic commands, you can venture into more advanced training like agility, therapy work, and more. Labradoodles are known for their agility and quick learning abilities, making them great contenders for dog sports.

Did you know? Labradoodles have been successfully trained as guide dogs, therapy dogs, and other types of assistance dogs due to their intelligence, trainability, and friendly disposition!

Making Training Sessions Enjoyable

Training should be fun for your Labradoodle. Keep sessions short, positive, and rewarding. Mix training exercises with games to keep your Labradoodle interested and looking forward to their training sessions.

Early Recognition and Management of Behavioral Issues

It's crucial to identify and address behavioral issues early. Look out for signs of aggression, fear, anxiety, and destructive behaviors. These might require professional intervention. However, with patience, consistency, and positive reinforcement, most behavioral issues can be managed successfully.

Conclusion

Remember, every Labradoodle is unique, and what works for one might not work for another. It's all about understanding your pet, being patient, and providing them with lots of love and positive reinforcement. Training your Labradoodle doesn't just make them more obedient; it can also be a fun bonding experience that brings you even closer together. Happy training!

CHAPTER 7

Nutrition: Diet, Hydration, and Health

Understanding the Role of Nutrition in Your Labradoodle's Health

Feeding your Labradoodle a balanced, nutritious diet is one of the most crucial aspects of ensuring their overall health and well-being. Nutrition affects everything from your dog's skin and coat to their energy levels, immune system, and even their mood. But just what constitutes a balanced diet for a Labradoodle?

Typically, a well-rounded Labradoodle diet should consist of high-quality protein (for muscle development and energy), carbohydrates (for quick energy), fats (for sustained energy and skin health), vitamins and minerals (for various bodily functions), and fiber (for digestive health).

Choosing the Right Food for Your Labradoodle

When selecting food for your Labradoodle, consider their age, size, and activity level. Puppies, adults, and seniors all have different nutritional needs. Puppies are growing rapidly and require food that's high in protein and calories. Adults need a balanced diet that keeps them fit and energetic without causing weight gain. Senior dogs often require fewer calories but more fiber and certain nutrients.

There are many types of dog food available on the market, including kibble, canned, raw, and homemade diets. Each type has its advantages and disadvantages.

Kibble is convenient, economical, and good for your dog's teeth due to the crunch factor, but it's essential to choose a premium brand that uses high-quality ingredients.

Canned food is usually higher in protein and very palatable to dogs. However, it can be expensive and may contribute to dental problems if not balanced with some dry food or dental chews.

Raw diets can offer a highly digestible, natural form of nutrition, but they can also be expensive, time-consuming to prepare, and carry risks if not properly balanced or handled safely.

Homemade diets give you control over what your dog is eating, but they require a lot of work and knowledge to ensure they're nutritionally complete.

A vet or a canine nutrition expert can help you choose the best diet for your Labradoodle.

Fun Fact: Did you know that the Labradoodle's ancestors, the Labrador Retriever and the Poodle, both come from working backgrounds? This means Labradoodles often have high energy needs and benefit from a diet rich in protein!

Recognizing Food Allergies and Intolerances

Like humans, dogs can suffer from food allergies and intolerances. Some Labradoodles may have sensitivities to certain ingredients like wheat, corn, or specific proteins. Symptoms can range from gastrointestinal upset (like diarrhea or vomiting) to skin issues (like itching or redness). If you notice these signs, it's important to consult with a vet. They may recommend an elimination diet to identify the problematic ingredient.

Preventing Obesity and Other Health Issues through Diet

A balanced diet can help prevent a variety of health issues, including obesity, which is a growing problem in dogs. Obesity can lead to serious health complications like diabetes, heart disease, and joint problems. Monitoring your Labradoodle's weight, feeding them the right amount, and ensuring they get plenty of exercises can prevent these issues.

Remember, while Labradoodles love to eat, it's your responsibility to control portion sizes. A handy tip: The amount of food recommended on dog food packaging is often more than many dogs need – these guidelines are meant to cover all dogs, including the most active ones. If in doubt, consult your vet about the best portion size for your Labradoodle.

Hydration: Keeping Your Labradoodle Refreshed

Hydration is just as important as diet. Always make sure your Labradoodle has access to fresh, clean water. A general rule of thumb is that dogs should drink about an ounce of water per pound of body weight each day. This amount will increase in hot weather or after exercise.

> Here's a quick tip: To check if your Labradoodle is hydrated, lift the skin on the back of their neck. If it springs back quickly, they're well hydrated. If it takes

a while to return to normal, they might need more water.

Understanding Food-Related Risks

It's also important to know what foods are harmful to dogs. Many human foods are toxic to them, including chocolate, onions, garlic, grapes, and raisins. Make sure to keep these foods out of your Labradoodle's reach.

It's not just food; certain plants, like some types of lilies and azaleas, can also be toxic. It's always a good idea to research whether the plants in your home and garden are dog-safe.

Catering to Your Labradoodle's Changing Nutritional Needs

As your Labradoodle ages, their nutritional needs will change. Puppies need lots of calories for growth, while seniors need fewer calories but more fiber and specific nutrients. Your vet can help you adjust your Labradoodle's diet to suit these changing needs, ensuring they stay healthy and happy throughout their life.

To sum it up, feeding your Labradoodle a balanced, age-appropriate diet and providing plenty of fresh water are crucial steps towards keeping them healthy. Always watch for signs of food allergies and monitor your Labradoodle's weight to prevent obesity.

Remember to adjust their diet as they age and consult your vet if you're ever unsure about your Labradoodle's nutritional needs.

CHAPTER 8

Exercise and Enrichment for Your Labradoodle

J ust like humans, dogs require both physical and mental exercise to lead a happy and balanced life. Labradoodles, with their heritage of athletic Retrievers and clever Poodles, especially thrive when given adequate outlets for their energy and intelligence.

Exercise Needs at Different Life Stages

Understanding the exercise needs of Labradoodles at different life stages is crucial. Puppies and young adults often have a lot of energy to burn off, while senior dogs may need gentler, more moderate exercise. Be aware that over-exercising a young puppy can lead to joint and bone problems in the future due to the stress it places on their developing bodies.

Tip: Labradoodle puppies need approximately five minutes of exercise per month of age, up to twice a day.

The Importance of Mental Stimulation

Labradoodles are highly intelligent dogs, which means they need plenty of mental stimulation to keep them engaged. This can be accomplished through training sessions, puzzle toys, interactive games, or even just a change in environment.

Did you know? Mental stimulation can tire a dog out just as much as physical exercise.

Forms of Exercise

Walks and runs are excellent forms of exercise for your Labradoodle. In addition, many Labradoodles love water and will enjoy swimming sessions. Playing games like fetch, frisbee, and tug-of-war are other fun ways to exercise. Dog sports such as agility, flyball, or dock diving can also be great outlets for their energy and intelligence.

Fun fact: The Poodle ancestors of Labradoodles were originally bred as water retrievers, which may explain your Labradoodle's love for swimming!

Indoor Fun and Games

It's important to have a range of toys and interactive activities for indoor fun, especially in inclement weather. This can include treat-dispensing toys, chew toys, or even a game of hide and seek.

Socialization and Exercise

Dog parks and other communal spaces can provide both socialization and exercise opportunities. However, it's important to supervise your Labradoodle in these situations to ensure they play nicely with others and don't become overwhelmed.

Tailoring Exercise to Your Labradoodle's Preferences

Just like people, dogs have their own preferences when it comes to exercise. Some may enjoy long runs, while others prefer a game of fetch. Experiment with different activities to find out what your Labradoodle enjoys the most.

Recognizing Over-Exertion

While exercise is important, it's equally crucial to avoid over-exertion. Watch out for signs such as excessive panting, limping, or reluctance to continue. Always ensure your Labradoodle has access to fresh water during and after exercise.

Balance Between Exercise and Rest

Just as exercise is crucial, so is rest. Make sure your Labradoodle has ample time to recuperate and rest, especially after a vigorous play session or workout.

Staying Active in Later Years

As your Labradoodle ages, their exercise needs may change, but they should remain active. Adapt their exercise routine to accommodate any health issues or mobility problems.

CHAPTER 9

Health and Wellness: Preventative Care, Common Issues, and Vet Visits

I n this chapter, we'll delve into the vital subject of Labradoodle health and wellness. From preventative care measures to recognizing common health issues, this chapter serves as your comprehensive guide. Regular vet visits and the importance of addressing health concerns promptly will also be covered, ensuring that your furry friend stays in tip–top condition throughout their lifetime.

Common Health Issues in Labradoodles: Understanding Labradoodle–Specific Health Concerns

Labradoodles, like any breed, have a set of health concerns that are more common within the breed.

Hip and Elbow Dysplasia

Both conditions are hereditary and cause abnormal development in the respective joints, leading to discomfort, pain, and mobility issues. Hip dysplasia is especially prevalent among larger dogs, while elbow dysplasia affects dogs of all sizes.

Eye Disorders

Labradoodles are prone to several eye disorders, including progressive retinal atrophy (PRA), cataracts, and glaucoma. Regular eye checks can help to detect these conditions early, often before they cause significant vision impairment.

Addison's Disease

This condition occurs when the adrenal glands fail to produce adequate amounts of certain hormones. Symptoms can be vague and can include fatigue, weakness, loss of appetite, and depression.

Recognizing Symptoms

Recognizing the early signs of these common health conditions can help ensure your Labradoodle gets the right treatment promptly. Watch for symptoms such as limping, difficulty moving, changes in behavior, excessive thirst, changes in weight, and cloudy or red eyes.

Regular Vet Check-ups and Vaccinations

The Importance of Regular Vet Visits

Regular vet check-ups are essential for monitoring your Labradoodle's overall health. These visits allow the vet to detect any potential health problems early.

Labradoodle Vaccination Schedule

Your Labradoodle should receive their initial set of vaccinations between six to eight weeks of age, with booster shots given every three to four weeks until they are about four months old. After this, most vaccinations are done annually or every three years, depending on the specific vaccine.

Understanding When to Seek Veterinary Care

Labradoodles, like all dogs, can experience illnesses and injuries. Recognizing when your Labradoodle needs veterinary care is critical. Signs of distress can include sudden changes in behavior, lack of appetite, increased thirst, labored breathing, persistent vomiting or diarrhea, unexplained weight loss, and disorientation.

Preventing Parasites

Labradoodles can be susceptible to various parasites, including fleas, ticks, and heartworms.

Flea and Tick Prevention

Monthly topical treatments or oral medications can help keep these external parasites at bay.

Heartworm Prevention

Heartworms are transmitted through mosquito bites and can cause severe and potentially fatal heart and lung damage. Monthly preventative medications are a must.

Dental Care for Your Labradoodle

Regular brushing and dental chews can help maintain your Labradoodle's oral health. Labradoodles, like many breeds, can be prone to dental diseases such as periodontal disease and gingivitis if their oral health is not properly maintained.

Eye and Ear Care

Eye Care

Regularly check your Labradoodle's eyes for signs of redness, irritation, or discharge.

Ear Care

Labradoodles have floppy ears that can be prone to infection. Regular cleaning and drying, especially after swimming, can help prevent these issues.

Weight Management and the Risks of Obesity

Obesity can lead to numerous health issues, including diabetes, heart disease, and joint problems. A balanced diet and regular exercise are key to maintaining your Labradoodle's ideal weight.

Genetic Testing for Health Conditions

Genetic testing can be a valuable tool in identifying potential health issues, especially for breeds like the Labradoodle, which can be prone to certain genetic conditions.

Senior Care

As your Labradoodle ages, their health care needs will change. Regular vet check-ups become even more important, and adjustments may need to be made to their diet and exercise regimen.

Remember, your vet is your partner in ensuring your Labradoodle's health and wellbeing. Don't hesitate to reach out with any questions or concerns you may have. After all, no one knows your Labradoodle better than you do!

> Did you know? Labradoodles are known for their long lifespan compared to other breeds of similar size. With proper care and attention to their health, Labradoodles can live into their early teens and even longer.

In the next chapter, we will dive deeper into grooming techniques to keep your Labradoodle looking their best and keeping their coat healthy.

CHAPTER 10

Grooming: Mastering the Art of Coat Care

The Importance of Grooming

Just like nutrition, grooming plays a significant role in your Labradoodle's overall health and well-being. Regular grooming helps keep your Labradoodle clean, reduces the amount of hair shed around your home, and provides an opportunity to spot any abnormalities (like lumps, ticks, or skin problems) early.

Labradoodles have a unique coat that can vary from wavy to curly. Thanks to their Poodle heritage, many Labradoodles are low-shedding, making them an excellent choice for those with allergies. However, this low-shedding coat needs specific care to keep it looking its best.

Tools for Grooming Your Labradoodle

Before you begin grooming your Labradoodle, it's essential to gather the right tools. Here are some of the must-haves for your grooming kit:

1. Brush: A slicker brush works well for most Labradoodle coats. It can effectively remove loose hair and detangle knots.

2. Comb: A steel comb is beneficial for getting through thick coats and tackling stubborn tangles.

3. Dog Shampoo and Conditioner: Look for a gentle dog shampoo that's free of harsh chemicals. A dog-specific conditioner can help keep your Labradoodle's coat soft and manageable.

4. Dog Hair Clippers: If you plan to do haircuts at home, investing in a good pair of dog hair clippers can save you lots of time and effort.

5. Nail Clippers or Grinder: Regular nail trims are essential for your Labradoodle's comfort and health. Whether you prefer clippers or a grinder will depend on your and your dog's comfort levels.

6. Ear Cleaning Solution: Labradoodles' floppy ears can be prone to infection. Regular cleaning with a vet-recommended solution can help prevent this.

Labradoodles are known for their stunning, wavy coats, a unique blend of their Labrador Retriever and Poodle lineage. These coats can range from straight, wavy, to tightly curled, and each type comes with its specific grooming needs.

Understanding the Different Coat Types in Labradoodles: Wool, Fleece, and Hair

Just like humans, Labradoodles can have different types of hair. Understanding these differences is crucial in providing the right grooming care.

Wool Coat

Wool coats are similar to Poodles, characterized by tight curls. This type of coat is low-shedding, making it an excellent choice for those with allergies. However, the wool coat requires regular grooming to prevent matting and tangling.

Fleece Coat

Fleece coats are a mix between the Poodle's curly coat and the Labrador's straight coat, resulting in a wavy or loose curl pattern. This type of coat is also low-shedding and allergy-friendly. It requires less maintenance than the wool coat but still needs regular grooming to stay healthy.

Hair Coat

Hair coats, often found in first-generation (F1) Labradoodles, are similar to those of Labrador Retrievers. This type of coat sheds more than the wool and fleece types, and it may trigger allergies. However, it is the easiest to maintain when it comes to grooming.

The Importance of Regular Grooming for Labradoodles

Proper grooming is about more than just keeping your Labradoodle looking good; it's about their overall health and well-being too. Regular grooming helps keep your dog's skin healthy by stimulating blood flow and distributing natural oils. It allows you to check for any abnormalities, like skin issues, parasites, lumps, or injuries. Plus, grooming sessions provide an excellent opportunity to bond with your furry friend.

Basics of Brushing, Bathing, and Nail Trimming

Brushing

Regardless of the coat type, all Labradoodles need regular brushing to prevent matting and keep their coats healthy.

For wool and fleece-coated Labradoodles, daily brushing may be necessary to avoid tangles. Use a slicker brush or a comb designed for long-haired dogs, working gently to avoid hurting your dog's skin. Make sure to get down to the undercoat, as this is where most of the tangling occurs.

For hair-coated Labradoodles, brushing every few days is sufficient. A bristle brush or a rubber grooming mitt works well for this type of coat.

Did you know? Brushing not only keeps your Labradoodle's coat looking good but it's also a great way to check for any skin issues, ticks, or fleas!

Bathing

Bathing is an important part of grooming, but it should not be overdone. Labradoodles should generally be bathed once every three months, or when they get particularly dirty. Overbathing can lead to dry skin and coat problems.

Always use a dog-friendly shampoo and conditioner that matches your Labradoodle's skin type. After lathering the shampoo, make sure to rinse thoroughly, as leftover shampoo can cause skin irritation.

Nail Trimming

Keeping your Labradoodle's nails trimmed is essential to their comfort and health. Untrimmed nails can cause discomfort and affect your dog's gait, leading to long-term health issues. Aim to trim your Labradoodle's nails every 4-6 weeks. If you can hear their nails clicking on the floor, it's time for a trim!

Professional Grooming Needs and Frequency

While regular at-home grooming is vital, professional grooming sessions can be beneficial, especially for Labradoodles with wool or fleece coats. Professional groomers are trained to handle more complex tasks like ear cleaning, anal gland expression, and haircutting.

Most Labradoodles benefit from professional grooming every 6–8 weeks. This frequency can vary based on the type and condition of your Labradoodle's coat, their age, and their activity level.

Dealing with Seasonal Shedding and Coat Changes

Labradoodles with hair coats will experience seasonal shedding, while those with wool or fleece coats will shed minimally. During shedding season, typically in the spring and fall, increased brushing can help manage the loose fur.

Labradoodle puppies are born with a soft puppy coat that starts changing around 6–12 months of age. This is when the adult coat comes in and can be a challenging time in terms of grooming. Regular brushing and perhaps more frequent professional grooming can help manage this transition phase.

Tips to Keep Your Labradoodle's Coat Healthy and Shiny

A Labradoodle's coat can be a reflection of their overall health. A balanced diet rich in Omega-3 and Omega-6 fatty acids can promote a shiny and healthy coat. Regular exercise also stimulates blood flow to the skin, contributing to a healthier coat.

Another tip to maintain your Labradoodle's coat health is to always dry them properly after a bath or a swim. Excessive moisture can lead to skin issues, such as hot spots.

Special Grooming Considerations for Puppies and Senior Dogs

Labradoodle puppies and seniors require extra attention during grooming. Puppies, especially those undergoing a coat change, need frequent brushing to prevent tangles and matting. Grooming sessions are also an excellent opportunity to acclimate your puppy to being handled, a skill that will be beneficial throughout their life.

Senior Labradoodles may have more sensitive skin and may be prone to skin issues. Regular gentle brushing helps stimulate blood flow and keep the skin healthy. Also, as senior dogs can be less active, their nails might require more frequent trimming.

Conclusion

Grooming your Labradoodle is a rewarding task that contributes significantly to their overall health and well-being. Although it may seem daunting at first, with practice, patience, and the right tools, you can master the art of Labradoodle grooming. Remember that each Labradoodle is unique, and their grooming needs may vary. Adjust your grooming routine as needed, and always make the process enjoyable for your furry friend.

Pro tip: Keep treats handy during grooming sessions. They can serve as a distraction during tricky moments and as a reward for your Labradoodle's cooperation.

CHAPTER 11

Exercise and Play: Ensuring Physical and Mental Stimulation

There's a popular saying among Labradoodle owners: *"A tired Labradoodle is a good Labradoodle."* This isn't a negative comment on the breed; rather, it highlights one of their most distinguishing characteristics – their abundant energy and need for physical and mental stimulation.

Your Labradoodle's zest for life is one of the things you'll love the most about them. But remember, an under-stimulated, bored Labradoodle can resort to destructive behavior like chewing furniture or excessive barking. But fear not, this chapter is here to guide you on how to keep your Labradoodle happy, healthy, and mentally stimulated.

Understanding Labradoodle's Energy Levels

Labradoodles are known for their exuberance and high energy levels. Born from a line of working dogs – the Labrador Retriever and the Poodle – these dogs are athletic, intelligent, and always up for an adventure.

The Labrador parent was historically bred for physically demanding jobs, like retrieving fishing nets, while the Poodle was a hunting dog that loved water. These traits contribute to the Labradoodle's love for exercise and play.

Generally, Labradoodles need around an hour to an hour and a half of exercise daily. However, this can vary based on their age, health, and individual temperament. Puppies have bursts of high energy and require short, frequent play sessions, while older dogs may be content with a leisurely walk and a short game of fetch.

A helpful tip: Always monitor your dog during exercise. Panting is normal, but if they seem overly tired or don't want to play, it's time to take a break.

Keeping Your Labradoodle Mentally Stimulated

Remember, Labradoodles aren't just physically active – they're mentally agile too. They inherit their intelligence from their Poodle parent, who is ranked as the second most intelligent dog breed. Engaging their mind is as important as providing them with physical exercise.

Interactive toys are a fantastic way to keep your Labradoodle's mind active. Puzzle toys, where they have to work out how to get to a treat, can keep them busy for a good while. Training sessions also serve as excellent mental exercise. Teaching them new commands or tricks can be a fun and rewarding way to stimulate their mind.

Labradoodles and Water: Introducing Safe Swimming Activities

Labradoodles often inherit a love for water from their Labrador Retriever parent. Swimming is a great exercise for them, and it's also a fun way to cool down on a hot day.

If you have access to a safe body of water, such as a dog-friendly beach or a shallow lake, or even a doggy pool in your backyard, these can be excellent options for your Labradoodle to paddle. Remember to introduce them to water gradually and always supervise swimming sessions for safety.

Interactive Games and Toys Suitable for Labradoodles

Playtime is a crucial aspect of your Labradoodle's exercise routine. Interactive games can provide both physical exercise and mental stimulation.

Fetch is a favorite game for many Labradoodles due to their retriever instincts. Use a variety of objects - balls, frisbees, or dog-safe plush toys, to keep it interesting. "Hide and Seek" can be another fun game. You can hide their favorite toy or treat and let them find it. This not only provides physical exercise but also engages their sense of smell, providing mental stimulation.

Toys that dispense treats when interacted with can keep your Labradoodle occupied for hours. Just remember to account for these treats in their daily food intake to prevent overfeeding.

Training Your Labradoodle for Dog Sports

Dog sports like agility, rally, and obedience trials are not just for show dogs; they can be an exciting and enriching experience for any dog, including your Labradoodle.

Agility, where dogs navigate a course with various obstacles, can be a fantastic outlet for their energy and intelligence. Rally is a sport that involves obedience and agility elements, requiring strong communication between you and your dog. It's a team sport, which can strengthen your bond with your Labradoodle.

Getting involved in these sports doesn't mean you have to compete. Many dog owners train for these sports purely for fun and the benefits it brings to their dogs.

Keeping Your Labradoodle Entertained Indoors

You might not always have the option to take your Labradoodle out for exercise, like during inclement weather or when they're recovering from an illness. In such cases, it's good to have indoor activities ready to keep them entertained.

> Did you know you can play indoor fetch? Using a soft toy and throwing it down a corridor can work well. Puzzle toys, as mentioned earlier, can be another lifesaver. Teaching your Labradoodle new tricks or reinforcing old ones can also be a great indoor activity.

Adjusting Exercise Routines as Your Labradoodle Ages

As your Labradoodle grows older, their exercise needs will change. They may not be able to handle the long runs or intense games of fetch that they enjoyed in their youth. However, they still need regular, gentle exercise to keep them fit and prevent obesity.

Shorter, more frequent walks can be beneficial for older Labradoodles. Swimming can be another excellent low-impact exercise for senior dogs if it's an activity they enjoy.

Keep an eye on your dog during exercise, and if they seem to be struggling, it's time to take a break. Regular vet check-ups are essential to monitor their health and adjust their exercise routine as necessary.

Your Labradoodle is a bundle of energy, ready to explore the world with you. Balancing physical exercise with mental stimulation will ensure they are content, well-behaved, and healthy. So, strap on those walking shoes, grab a few toys, and get ready for the exciting journey of keeping up with your Labradoodle!

Remember, every Labradoodle is an individual. What works for one might not work for another. Your bond with your Labradoodle will help you understand their unique needs and preferences, guiding you to provide them with the best care possible.

CHAPTER 12

Behavior and Training: From Puppyhood to Adulthood

Understanding the Labradoodle Temperament

The Labradoodle is a blend of two of the world's smartest breeds: the Labrador Retriever and the Poodle. This heritage has blessed the Labradoodle with a dynamic temperament. Labradoodles are known for being intelligent, playful, affectionate, and sociable. They usually get along well with children and other pets, making them excellent family dogs. Labradoodles are eager to please, which combined with their high intelligence, makes them highly trainable. However, their spirited personalities can sometimes lead to mischievousness or stubbornness.

> **Did You Know?** The term 'Labradoodle' was first used in 1955, but the breed didn't gain popularity until the 1980s when an Australian breeder started breeding them as hypoallergenic guide dogs.

The Importance of Early Socialization and Training

Socialization is crucial for all dogs, but it is particularly vital for intelligent breeds like the Labradoodle. Lack of exposure to different environments, people, and animals during the early months can lead to fear-based behaviors or aggression later in life.

A properly socialized Labradoodle is confident, friendly, and well-adjusted. You should introduce your puppy to a variety of people, dogs, and environments to ensure they grow up to be sociable and well-behaved. Remember to always make these experiences positive. Reward your Labradoodle with treats, praises, and petting, so they associate new experiences with positive outcomes.

Fun Fact: Dogs have a primary socialization period that lasts from about 3 weeks to 3 months of age. This period is when your puppy is most open to learning and forming relationships, making it the perfect time for socialization.

Training should begin as soon as your Labradoodle puppy comes home. Start with basic commands like "sit," "stay," and "come." You will be surprised at how quickly they catch on due to their intelligence.

Dealing with Common Behavioral Issues Specific to Labradoodles

Labradoodles are generally well-behaved, but like any breed, they can develop behavioral issues if not properly trained and socialized. Let's look at some common issues:

1. **Jumping on People:** Labradoodles are enthusiastic and sociable dogs, and this can sometimes lead to jumping behavior. It's crucial to discourage this behavior early on, as it can be problematic when your Labradoodle grows to their full size of up to 24 inches (61 centimeters) tall and 65 pounds (29.5 kilograms). Redirect their energy to a more appropriate greeting behavior, like sitting, and reward them for it.

2. **Chewing:** Labradoodles, especially puppies, love to chew. Provide plenty of chew toys and redirect them towards these toys if you catch them chewing on something inappropriate. If

the chewing is excessive, it could be due to teething, boredom, or anxiety.

3. Barking: Some Labradoodles can be quite vocal. While this trait can make them good watchdogs, excessive barking can become a nuisance. Training your dog the "quiet" command can help manage this behavior.

4. Separation Anxiety: Labradoodles love their human family and can become anxious when left alone for extended periods. To prevent this, gradually increase the amount of time you leave your dog alone, starting from a few minutes to several hours. Providing puzzle toys or Kongs filled with treats can keep them occupied while you're away.

Remember: Always use positive reinforcement methods when dealing with behavioral issues. Punishing your dog can lead to fear and anxiety, which may worsen the problem.

Teaching Obedience Commands and Tricks: The Labradoodle Way

Labradoodles are intelligent and eager to please, which makes them a joy to train. Start with basic commands like "sit," "stay," "down," and "leave it." Once your Labradoodle has mastered these, you can move on to more advanced tricks.

Training sessions should be short and fun. Use lots of positive reinforcement, including treats, praises, and petting. Be consistent with your commands and rewards, and always end the session on a positive note.

> Tip: "Labradoodles love using their brains. To keep training engaging, introduce puzzle games or try teaching them fun tricks like 'play dead' or 'spin.'"

House Training and Crate Training Strategies

House training is one of the first things you'll want to work on with your Labradoodle puppy. Establish a routine and take them out frequently, especially after meals, playtime, and naps. Always reward them when they do their business outside.

Crate training is another essential task. When done correctly, the crate becomes a safe and comfortable space for your dog. Introduce the crate gradually and make it a positive experience. Feed your Labradoodle in their crate, and provide treats and toys inside the crate. Never use the crate as punishment.

Utilizing the Labradoodle's Intelligence in Advanced Training Activities

Given their intelligence and agility, Labradoodles can excel at advanced training activities such as agility, obedience, and rally trials. These activities can provide excellent mental and physical stimulation for your Labradoodle. However, ensure your dog is physically mature before beginning strenuous activities to prevent injuries.

Understanding the "Adolescent Phase" in Labradoodles and How to Manage It

Just like human teenagers, dogs go through an adolescent phase, too. This phase typically begins around six months and can last until the dog is two years old. During this time, your previously obedient Labradoodle might start testing boundaries and ignoring commands.

Don't worry! Stay consistent with your training, provide plenty of exercise to help manage their increased energy levels, and most importantly, be patient. This phase will pass, and with the right guidance, your Labradoodle will transition into a well-behaved adult dog.

Patience and Consistency Are Key

Training your Labradoodle requires patience, consistency, and understanding. Remember, every dog is unique and progresses at their own pace. Don't be discouraged if your Labradoodle takes longer to grasp certain commands or behaviors. With your guidance and dedication, your Labradoodle will grow up to be a well-rounded and well-behaved member of your family.

Quote to Remember: "A dog is the only thing on earth that loves you more than he loves himself." – Josh Billings

Enjoy every moment of the journey, because the bond you're building with your Labradoodle through training is truly special.

CHAPTER 13

The Aging Labradoodle: Ensuring a Comfortable and Joyful Senior Life

J ust as we humans age, so do our four-legged friends. Labradoodles, with their love for play and energetic spirit, can seem forever young, but inevitably, they too experience the effects of aging. This chapter provides comprehensive information on understanding and caring for your senior Labradoodle, helping them transition smoothly into their golden years.

Understanding the Lifespan of a Labradoodle and What Constitutes 'Senior'

Labradoodles, as a breed, have a relatively long lifespan com-
pared to other dog breeds. On average, they live between 10 to 15
years, though some may live even longer with proper care and
good genetics. While age is not the sole determinant, a Labradoodle is generally considered a 'senior' around the age of 7 to 8 years.

> Tip: Keep in mind that each dog ages differently, and
> factors such as size, health, and genetics can influence
> when your Labradoodle starts to show signs of aging.

Adjusting to Age-Related Changes

Like humans, senior dogs undergo physical and mental
changes. It's essential to note these changes and adapt their care
routine accordingly.

Physical Changes and Health Concerns

As your Labradoodle ages, you may notice some physical
changes. These can include graying fur, especially around the
muzzle, decreased activity levels, weight gain or loss, and the

development of lumps or bumps under the skin. Hearing and vision may start to decline, and their movements may slow down due to arthritis or other joint issues.

It's crucial to monitor your senior Labradoodle's health closely and schedule regular vet check-ups. Older dogs are more prone to certain health problems like heart disease, kidney disease, diabetes, and cancer. However, early detection and treatment can significantly improve the prognosis for these conditions.

Diet and Nutrition

As Labradoodles get older, their dietary needs also change. Aging dogs usually require fewer calories as their metabolism slows down, but they still need a diet rich in high-quality proteins and certain nutrients to support joint health and overall well-being.

Speak with your vet to develop a diet plan that suits your senior Labradoodle's needs. They may recommend a diet specifically formulated for senior dogs, or they might suggest dietary supplements to support joint health and digestion.

Exercise and Mobility

While senior Labradoodles might not have the same energy levels as they did in their younger years, regular exercise remains crucial to keep them healthy and happy. You might need to adjust the intensity and duration of their activity—longer, leisurely walks might replace strenuous runs, for example.

It's not uncommon for senior dogs to develop arthritis or other joint issues, which can impact their mobility. If you notice your Labradoodle struggling to move, experiencing discomfort during or after exercise, or showing reluctance to engage in activities they previously enjoyed, it's time to consult your vet.

Mental Health and Enrichment

Cognitive decline is another aspect of aging, seen even in dogs. This can manifest as confusion, disorientation, decreased activity, changes in sleeping patterns, or even behavioral changes.

To keep your Labradoodle's mind sharp, continue to provide mental stimulation through interactive games, puzzles, or new learning exercises. Even simple activities like a new walking route or interacting with a new toy can help stimulate their mind.

Caring for Your Senior Labradoodle's Specific Needs

As your Labradoodle enters their senior years, their care routine needs to be adjusted to suit their changing needs.

Regular Vet Check-ups and Preventative Care for Senior Dogs

Senior dogs should visit the vet at least twice a year, even if they appear healthy. Regular check-ups can help detect potential health problems early. Your vet will likely conduct a comprehensive physical examination, including blood work, urinalysis, and other diagnostic tests to evaluate your dog's health.

Vaccinations, parasite control, and dental care remain essential components of preventative care. Dental disease is especially common in older dogs, so maintaining good oral hygiene through regular brushing and dental chews is important. Your vet might also recommend more frequent professional dental cleanings.

Did you know? An estimated 85% of all dogs have some form of dental disease by the time they are 3 years old, and this risk only increases as they age.

Comfort Considerations: Sleeping Arrangements, Mobility, and More

As dogs age, they may need more rest than they did in their youthful years. Make sure your Labradoodle has a comfortable, warm, and quiet place to relax. Orthopedic beds can provide extra support for arthritic dogs.

Mobility can be an issue for senior dogs. If your Labradoodle has trouble getting around—perhaps they can't climb stairs as they used to or struggle to hop into the car—consider using ramps or stairs to help them. Slipping on hard floors can also be a problem, so use non–slip rugs or mats in frequently used areas.

If your Labradoodle has developed incontinence or other age–related issues, you may need to adjust your home accordingly. This could involve using pet diapers or pads and ensuring they have easy access to their toilet area.

Grieving and Pet Loss: Coming to Terms with the End of the Journey

Finally, it's important to discuss a part of pet ownership that many people find hard to talk about: the end of life. Saying good–bye to a beloved pet is never easy, but understanding that it's a part of the natural life cycle can help you navigate this difficult time.

When the time comes, make sure your Labradoodle is comfortable and surrounded by love. Euthanasia, when necessary, should be a peaceful process conducted by a compassionate professional.

After your pet's passing, it's essential to allow yourself time to grieve. Everyone handles grief differently, and there's no right or wrong way to process the loss. Consider joining a pet loss support group, either in your local community or online, to share your feelings with others who understand your pain.

In the end, remember all the love and joy your Labradoodle brought to your life. They may be gone, but their memories will live on in your heart forever.

Entering the senior years doesn't mean the end of fun and happiness for your Labradoodle. With your love, care, and a few adjustments to their routine, these golden years can be a special time, filled with comfort and joy. It's a time to cherish your loyal friend, celebrating the bond you share, and ensuring their happiness for as long as possible.

CHAPTER 14

Labradoodles as Therapy and Service Dogs: Harnessing their Potential

In our journey of understanding and appreciating Labradoodles, it's important to acknowledge one of the most crucial
roles they play: as therapy and service dogs. This chapter ex-
plores the qualities that make Labradoodles excellent therapy
and service dogs, provides insight into the training and certification process, shares real-life stories of Labradoodles making a

difference, and discusses the responsibilities of owning a therapy or service Labradoodle.

Labradoodles: Born to Serve and Provide Comfort

1. What Makes Labradoodles Exceptional Therapy and Service Dogs

The wonderful blend of the Labrador Retriever's sociability and the Poodle's high intelligence makes the Labradoodle a natural fit for therapy and service work. Their intuitive nature and ability to empathize with human emotions set them apart. They're also known for their low-shedding coats, a boon for people with allergies.

> Did You Know? The Labradoodle was originally bred in the 1980s by Wally Conron, who was aiming to create a hypoallergenic guide dog for a blind woman whose husband was allergic to dogs.

2. Physical Traits That Support Their Roles

Labradoodles' size ranges from medium to large (between 14 and 24 inches in height and 15 to 65 pounds or 7 to 29 kilograms in weight), making them sturdy enough to perform physical tasks without being overly imposing or difficult to manage. Their high energy levels and good health make them excellent working dogs.

3. Temperamental Traits Suited for Therapy and Service

Labradoodles are generally friendly, patient, and trainable—traits that are critical in therapy and service dogs. They are also exceptionally intuitive, which aids in understanding and responding to human emotions and commands.

The Path to Certification: Training Your Labradoodle for Therapy and Service Roles

1. Understanding the Difference: Therapy Dogs vs Service Dogs

It's vital to understand that therapy dogs and service dogs serve different roles. While both contribute significantly to human health and happiness, service dogs are trained to perform specific tasks for individuals with disabilities, whereas therapy dogs provide comfort and emotional support in various settings.

2. Preparing for Training

Before you embark on the training journey, make sure your Labradoodle is in good health. Regular vet check-ups and a balanced diet are crucial. A Labradoodle chosen for service or therapy work must also have a naturally calm demeanor and be comfortable in a variety of environments.

3. Training a Therapy Dog

Training for a therapy dog primarily focuses on basic obedience and socialization. Commands such as 'sit,' 'stay,' 'down,' 'come,' and 'leave it' are essential. Dogs must be comfortable being petted and handled, even clumsily, as they could be working with children or individuals with motor skill difficulties.

4. Training a Service Dog

Service dog training is more intensive and specific than therapy dog training. The dog is trained to perform tasks like opening doors, fetching items, or even detecting a medical emergency like a seizure. This training is usually personalized to the needs of the individual the dog will be serving.

5. Certification Process

Both therapy and service dogs need to be certified by recognized organizations. For therapy dogs, organizations like Therapy Dogs International or Pet Partners offer certification programs. Service dogs are typically certified through specific training organizations that focus on the individual needs of the handler.

Labradoodles Making a Difference: Inspiring Stories

1. The Tale of Sandy: The Hospital Comforter

Sandy, a cream-colored Labradoodle, has been a therapy dog at the children's ward of a New York hospital for over six years. She has a knack for sensing distress and knows how to calm a child undergoing a difficult procedure or dealing with the stress of a hospital stay. Sandy's owner says, *"She doesn't just bring joy; she brings a sense of home and normalcy to these kids."*

2. The Story of Max: The PTSD Service Dog

Max, a chocolate Labradoodle, works as a service dog for a veteran diagnosed with PTSD. He's been trained to detect early signs of anxiety and distress in his owner. When Max senses escalating tension, he nudges his owner's hand with his nose—a cue that encourages grounding techniques to stave off a potential PTSD episode.

The Responsibility of Owning a Therapy or Service Labradoodle

1. Understanding the Commitment

Owning a service or therapy Labradoodle is a significant commitment. These dogs require regular training and mental stimulation due to their active roles. Regular health checks are also essential given their high activity levels.

2. The Importance of Public Etiquette

Service and therapy dogs must be well-behaved in public places, from stores to hospitals. As the owner, you must ensure your dog's behavior remains impeccable in all situations.

3. Recognizing the Balance Between Work and Play

While your Labradoodle may be a service or therapy dog, they're also a pet. They need time to unwind, play, and simply be a dog. Ensuring they have this balance is a vital part of being a responsible owner.

Labradoodles, with their perfect blend of charm, intelligence, and empathy, are indeed excellent candidates for therapy and service roles. Their roles as therapy and service dogs are a testament to their adaptability and the depth of their bond with humans. While it requires commitment and responsibility, raising a Labradoodle for these roles can be a rewarding experience filled with love and mutual respect.

CHAPTER 15

Labradoodle Q&A: Addressing Common Questions and Concerns

A s a Labradoodle owner or prospective owner, it's quite likely you've encountered numerous questions about this charming breed. In this chapter, we'll tackle some of the most frequently asked questions about Labradoodles, addressing common concerns about their behavior, health, and care. This chapter aims to dispel myths and misconceptions about Labradoodles, providing reliable information and resources for further learning.

Labradoodle 101: The Basics

What exactly is a Labradoodle?

A Labradoodle is a crossbreed dog, created by crossing a Labrador Retriever and a Poodle. They were initially bred in Australia in the 1980s with the goal of creating a guide dog suitable for people with allergies, as Poodles are known for their hypoallergenic coats.

> Fun fact: Did you know that the first Labradoodle was called "Sultan"? He successfully became a guide dog for a woman in Hawaii whose husband had severe allergies.

Are all Labradoodles hypoallergenic?

While Labradoodles are often marketed as hypoallergenic, it's important to note that no dog breed is truly hypoallergenic. Some Labradoodles may indeed have coats more suitable for people with allergies, particularly those with a higher percentage of Poodle genetics. But each dog is individual, and their allergenic properties can vary even within the same litter. If you have allergies, it's recommended to spend time with the specific Labradoodle before bringing it home.

Do Labradoodles shed?

Shedding in Labradoodles can vary greatly depending on the type of coat they inherit. Poodles are known for their minimal shedding, while Labradors are quite the opposite. Generally, Labradoodles with a higher percentage of Poodle genetics (like F1B or F2B generations) shed less than those with more Labrador genetics.

How big do Labradoodles get?

Labradoodles come in three main sizes: Miniature (about 14 to 16 inches tall at the shoulder, weighing between 15 to 25 pounds), Medium (18 to 20 inches tall, weighing between 30 to 45 pounds), and Standard (over 21 inches tall, usually weighing 50 to 65 pounds). The size primarily depends on the size of the Poodle parent.

Understanding Labradoodle Behavior

Are Labradoodles good family pets?

Yes, Labradoodles are often excellent family pets. They inherit the Labrador's friendly, outgoing nature, and the Poodle's intelligence and loyalty, making them sociable, smart, and generally good with children and other pets. However, individual behaviors can vary, and successful integration into a family depends on proper socialization, training, and a suitable environment.

> "Our Labradoodle, Charlie, has been a blessing to our family. He's patient with the kids, gets along with our cat, and always seems to know when one of us needs extra cuddles. He's not just a pet; he's a member of our family."

How much exercise does a Labradoodle need?

Labradoodles are active and energetic dogs that need regular exercise to stay happy and healthy. A good rule of thumb is at least 30 minutes to an hour of exercise per day, but this can vary based on their age, health, and individual energy levels. This exercise can be in the form of walks, playtime in the yard, or mental stimulation such as training exercises or puzzle toys.

Labradoodle Health Concerns

What health issues are common in Labradoodles?

As a mixed breed, Labradoodles can inherit health issues common to either Labradors or Poodles. This includes hip dysplasia, a variety of eye diseases, and in some cases, Addison's disease. Regular check-ups with a vet and genetic testing can help identify and manage these potential issues.

How long do Labradoodles live?

The average lifespan for a Labradoodle is around 12 to 14 years, although some have been known to live a few years longer with proper care and a healthy lifestyle. Regular veterinary care, a balanced diet, and plenty of exercises can contribute to a Labradoodle's longevity.

Labradoodle Care Essentials

How often should a Labradoodle be groomed?

Grooming frequency can depend on the type of coat your Labradoodle has. Those with hair or fleece-type coats, which are more Poodle-like, may need grooming every 6 to 8 weeks to prevent matting and tangling. Those with a more Labrador-like coat may require less frequent grooming. Regular brushing between grooming sessions is recommended for all Labradoodles.

What should I feed my Labradoodle?

Labradoodles should be fed high-quality dog food suitable for their size, age, and activity level. While some owners prefer dry kibble, others opt for canned, raw, or homemade diets. Regardless of your preference, it's crucial to ensure your Labradoodle's diet is balanced and nutritious. Always consult with a vet if you're considering significant dietary changes.

Did-you-know: While Labradoodles can thrive on various diets, did you know that sudden changes in their diet can lead to digestive upset? It's best to introduce new foods gradually over a week or so.

Final Thoughts

Remember, every Labradoodle is unique and may not fit the 'typical' mold. It's essential to understand their individual needs and traits, and to be prepared to provide them with the love, care, and commitment they deserve.

"Labradoodles are like a box of chocolates. You never know what you're going to get, but each one is a sweet surprise."

This chapter aimed to answer common questions about Labradoodles and offer guidance for potential concerns. But the learning doesn't stop here! As a responsible owner, it's essential to continue learning about your Labradoodle's needs, behaviors, and health considerations as they grow and develop.

Afterword

As we reach the end of "The Labradoodle Way: A Guide to Successful Dog Ownership," I hope you feel well-equipped and excited to embark on your incredible journey with your Labradoodle. From choosing your new best friend to ensuring their health and happiness throughout their life, we have covered a wide range of topics. In order to help you be the best possible Labradoodle owner, it has been my goal to give you a thorough, interesting, and enjoyable guide.

My Doodle, Isabel, has been a constant source of inspiration and happiness in my life, and I have faith that your Labradoodle will do the same for you. You should be able to forge a close bond with your Labradoodle while navigating the difficulties and rewards of dog ownership with the aid of the experiences I've shared in this book and the knowledge of veterinarians, cynologists, and canine behavior specialists.

Keep in mind that the foundations of a successful relationship with your Labradoodle are love, patience, and consistency. These principles will serve as your companion as you face new challenges, share experiences, and develop together.

Always consider the larger community as you travel with your Labradoodle. Clubs, organizations, and other Labradoodle enthusiasts can be great places to find support, friendship, and camaraderie. Share your experiences with others, gain knowledge from theirs, and keep learning more about the fascinating world of Labradoodles.

I'm thankful for the chance to share my love of Labradoodles with you and send you and your pet my best wishes for a lifetime of joy, amusement, and companionship. Remember to savor each moment because the years will fly by quickly and because each day offers fresh chances for development, education, and romance.

Thank you again for choosing 'The Labradoodle Way.' If you found this guide helpful, please consider leaving a review. Each review not only helps us to refine and enhance the book for future editions, but also helps fellow Labradoodle enthusiasts discover this resource.

Thank you for joining me on this incredible dog adventure! May "The Labradoodle Way" serve as a guiding light and a trusted resource throughout your journey with your cherished companion.

Sincerely,

Gus Tales and Isabel the Cavapoo

Acknowledgements

W e would like to extend our deepest gratitude to the numerous veterinary professionals, cynologists, and canine behavior therapists who lent their expertise to our Dog Life Series, and specifically, our work on Labradoodles. Special thanks to Dr. Richard Moss, Jan van Dam, Susan Thomas, and Eline van der Heijden for their invaluable insights and guidance.

We also owe a debt of gratitude to Doodle owners who took the time to read early versions of this book, including Alice Simmons, Mark Jensen, Dirk Janssens, and Anneke van der Meer. Their firsthand experiences and feedback significantly enriched this work.

To our family and friends, particularly Priscilla & Isabel, and Josh & Mark, thank you for your ongoing support and patience throughout this process.

Finally, we wish to acknowledge all dog lovers who share our passion for these beautiful creatures. This book is for you.